The Easter Story

Written by
Katherine Sully

Illustrated by
Simona Sanfilippo

QED Publishing

It was a long, dark night. Jesus was in trouble. Some people said he was the king of the Jews – King Herod didn't like it.

While Jesus prayed, Peter, James and John sat under the trees keeping watch.

This Book Belongs to:

....

Consultant: Fiona Moss, RE Adviser at RE Today Services
Editor: Cathy Jones
Designer: Chris Fraser
Editorial Assistant: Tasha Percy
Managing Editor: Victoria Garrard
Design Manager: Anna Lubecka

Copyright © QED Publishing 2013

First published in the UK in 2013 by
QED Publishing
A Quarto Group company
230 City Road
London EC1V 2TT

www.qed-publishing.co.uk

A catalogue record for this book is available
from the British Library.

ISBN 978 1 78171 177 4

Printed in China

But, one by one,
they fell asleep.

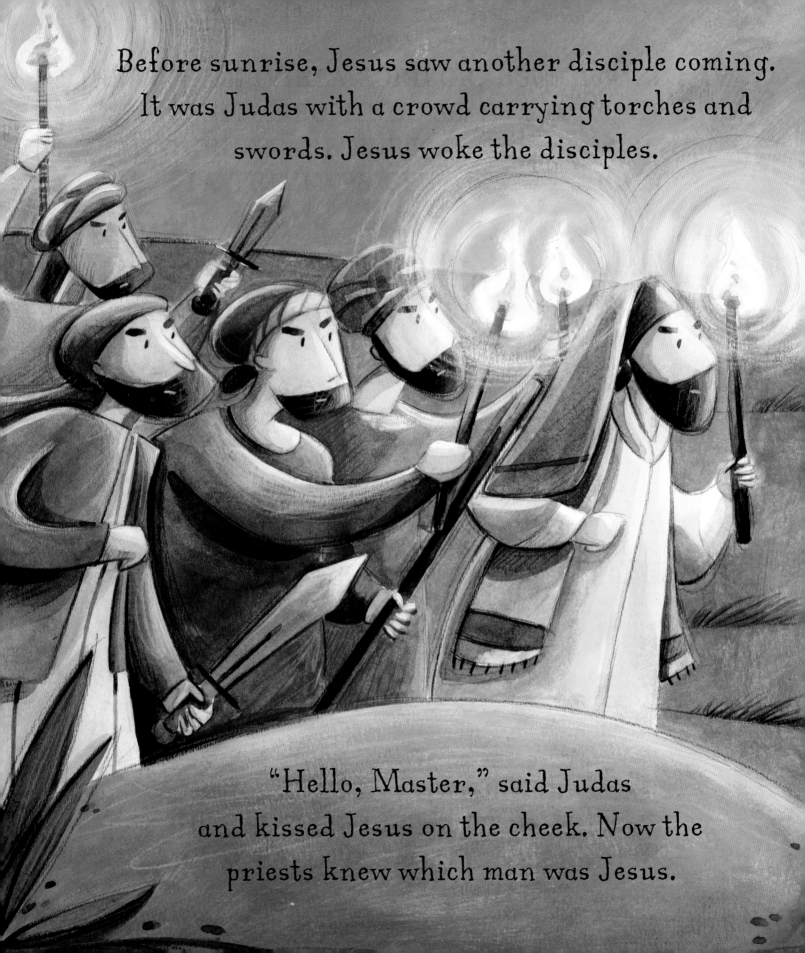

Before sunrise, Jesus saw another disciple coming. It was Judas with a crowd carrying torches and swords. Jesus woke the disciples.

"Hello, Master," said Judas and kissed Jesus on the cheek. Now the priests knew which man was Jesus.

Jesus was arrested. Peter swung his sword,
but Jesus told him not to fight.

Peter, James and
John ran away.

Jesus was taken to the chief priest. Peter had
followed and was listening from a safe distance.
But someone spotted him.

"You were with Jesus," they said.
"No I wasn't," said Peter. "I don't know him."

Three times Peter said he didn't know Jesus,
just as Jesus had said he would.

Cock-a-doodle-do! Then the cock crowed and
Peter cried because he hadn't
stood up for Jesus.

The priests took Jesus to Pilate, the Roman governor.
"Are you the king of the Jews?"
Pilate asked him. Jesus said nothing.

Pilate asked the crowd,
"What has he done?
He's hurt no one!"

But the crowd was angry.
"Who shall I let go?" asked Pilate. "Barabbas,
the murderer, or Jesus, king of the Jews?"

"Let Barabbas go!"
they cried.

Pilate was amazed, but
he let Barabbas go.

Boo!

Jesus was nailed to a wooden cross between two thieves. "If you are the Son of God," said the mean thief, "why don't you save yourself?"

"What has he done? He's hurt no one!" said the kind thief.

At midday, the sky went dark.
The darkness lasted for three hours.

"God, forgive them," Jesus cried.
"They don't know what they are doing!"

At the same moment, the earth rumbled and Jesus died.

A Roman soldier was standing guard. "He really was the Son of God," he said.

That evening, a man called Joseph took
Jesus' body to a stone tomb. He washed Jesus and
dressed him in clean clothes. Then he rolled a
heavy stone over the opening of the tomb.

Soldiers came to guard the tomb.

All this time, Jesus' friends, Mary Magdalene and Mary from Galilee, were watching.

Two days later,
Mary Magdalene and
Mary from Galilee came
back to the tomb.

The soldiers had gone,
the stone was rolled back
and the tomb was empty!

A shining angel said,
"Don't be afraid, Jesus is alive."

They ran quickly to tell the disciples.
But on the way, they met Jesus.

"Don't be afraid," said Jesus.
"I will meet the disciples in Galilee."

The disciples went to Galilee and waited. While they were talking, Jesus suddenly appeared. They were frightened!

"Why are you afraid?" asked Jesus. "It is me!"
He showed them the marks on his
hands and feet from the cross.

"Go and tell the world what
God has taught us: if we do
bad things, we should be sorry.
If other people do bad things
we should forgive them."

Jesus led his disciples to
a place near Bethany.

He lifted up his hands
and blessed them.
Jesus left them and was
taken up into heaven.

The disciples went out
into the world.
They spread God's message,
just as Jesus had told them.

Next Steps

Look back through the book to find more to talk about and join in with.

* Copy the actions. Do the actions with the characters – pray; draw your sword; roll the heavy stone.

* Join in with the rhyme. Pause to encourage joining in with
"What has he done?
He's hurt no one!"

* Count in fours. Count Jesus, Peter, James and John, count four torches, count the three women and John by the cross, count four doves.

* Name the colours. What colour clothes can you see in the crowd? Look back to spot the colours on other pages.

* All shapes and sizes. Look for big, middle-size and small trees.

* Listen to the noisy cockerel. When you see the word on the page, point and make the sound – Cock-a-doodle-do! Boo!

Now that you've read the story... what do you remember?

* Who led the crowd to Jesus?
* How many times did Peter say that he didn't know Jesus?
* What did the crowd put on Jesus' head?
* How did Jesus die?
* Where was Jesus buried?
* Who found out first that Jesus was alive?

What does the story tell us?
Jesus showed us that we should forgive other people, not blame them.